Phil Moser can be summed up in two words: biblical and practical. He is a master at applying the Scriptures to everyday issues in such a way that people walk away with lives changed.

KEVIN O'BRIAN
Pastor, Ocean City Baptist Church

Phil Moser has done an admirable job of identifying spiritual principles and then applying them to daily life. I commend this work both to those struggling with their daily walk, and to those counselors who are seeking additional tools.

DR. JOHN MACARTHUR
Pastor-Teacher, Grace Community Church
President, The Master's Seminary

Hats off to Phil Moser for helping us navigate through life's most challenging issues in a clearly biblical way. The thing I like about these booklets is that they are forged by a pastor who has successfully wrestled through these issues with his flock, and thankfully he now shares them with the church at large.

DR. JOE STOWELL
President, Cornerstone University

It has been a high privilege to know Phil Moser for more than 20 years. He is one of today's most gifted communicators; possessing an unusual ability to deliver biblical truth in an intensely personal and practical way. Our guests and students rate him a perennial favorite. I can give no higher recommendation for your next conference or speaking opportunity.

DON LOUGH
Executive Director, Word of Life Fellowship

Pastor Phil's writing reflects a deep commitment to helping individuals both understand and obey God's Word in their daily life. As an experienced counselor he realizes that just teaching the truth is not enough; people need help on the practical steps of disciplining themselves for the purpose of godliness. I commend this combination of exposition, call to obedience and "how-to."

RANDY PATTEN
Director of Training and Advancement
Association of Certified Biblical Counselors

As an educator, Phil Moser is distinctively gifted. His pedagogical skill enables him to clearly explain very difficult concepts in understandable language that all learners can grasp. Audiences would greatly benefit by his teaching.

CAROL A. SHARP, PH.D.
Served as Dean of the College of Education 2002-2012
Rowan University, Glassboro, New Jersey

I have been greatly encouraged by Phil's teaching. When I listen to him, I always walk away with more. More knowledge, more insight, more understanding, more hope. He's my go-to-guy when I have questions about the Bible or Christian living.

MICHAEL BOGGS
Singer-Songwriter
Winner of Multiple Dove Awards

The Biblical Strategies materials have been a big plus for our adult classes. With the inclusion of the memory verse packs and accountability study guides, the materials lend themselves readily to the discipleship process.

STEVE WILLOUGHBY
Pastor, First Baptist Church of Patchogue, New York

Taking Back Time

biblical strategies for overcoming procrastination

Phil Moser

Taking Back Time: biblical strategies for overcoming procrastination

Published by Biblical Strategies.
Distributed by Send the Light.

Visit our Web site: www.biblicalstrategies.com.

© 2014 Phil Moser
International Standard Book Number: 978-0-9905666-0-1

All rights reserved. No part of this book may be reproduced without prior written permission from the publisher, except where noted in the text and in the case of brief quotations embodied in critical articles and reviews.

Credits:
Cover Art: gracewaymedia.com, Gary Lizzi
Copy Editors: Wes Brown, Justin Carlton

Contributions:
Thanks to my dad, Arnie Moser (1925-2014), who modeled a love for the Word and devotion to learning that were inspirational.
Thanks to Joe Schenke for a message that generated the thoughts behind "Live by the Spirit" (pp. 41-56). His insights into "Roles with key Scriptures" was invaluable (p. 70).
Thanks to Jack Klose for the thought provoking questions that are a part of every accountability plan/study guide.

All Scripture quotations, unless otherwise indicated, are taken from THE HOLY BIBLE, English Standard Version. © 2001 Crossway Bibles, a ministry of Good News Publishers. Used by permission. All rights reserved.

Note: You may download a free accountability plan/study guide for *Taking Back Time* by visiting biblicalstrategies.com. Choose the resource tab to print the guide and other tools.

CONTENTS

Coming to Grips with Procrastination. 7

Part 1: Think like God Thinks. 9
Fear: the secret motivator
Pride: the overconfident optimist
Laziness: the stubborn enabler

Part 2: Do What Jesus Did 35
Rely on the Word, recite your purpose, rest in the Father,
reach for eternity

Part 3: Live by the Spirit 43
Analyze: Am I wasting time without realizing it?
Prioritize: Am I investing time in what is truly important?
Biblicize: Am I determining my priorities from Biblical values?
Exercise: Am I applying self-control with the use of my time?

Seeing Time as Stewardship 59

Practical Suggestions

Prayer
Prayer patterns & names of God 61

Bible Study
Key Bible passages on time & daily Bible reading plan 63

Scripture Retrieval
Scripture retrieval to overcome procrastination 66

Holy Spirit Dependence
The 15-minute journal. 68
The important/urgent matrix. 70
Roles with key Scriptures 72

COMING TO GRIPS WITH PROCRASTINATION

PROCRASTINATION. At five syllables, even the word takes a long time to say. Say it slowly and you're liable to evoke images of unbalanced checkbooks, people you meant to call back, and honey-do lists that have no end in sight. Each of us has a propensity to put off certain tasks. It's hard to pick up a book on procrastination, isn't it? Perhaps like me, you're afraid that you really weren't too busy to get to it, afraid that the problem really wasn't your schedule, afraid that you'll no longer be able to blame your boss. Too many discoveries like that, and you'll have to admit your need for change. And if you admit your need for change, that will be one more thing to put on the list. Of course, you could always put that off too.

We often limit our thoughts on procrastination to issues of time. We say, "I meant to get to that; I just didn't have enough time" or "Today was busy, so I had to put off that work until tomorrow." For this reason, most of the writing on procrastination will cover priorities or time-management. While this is important, the root cause lies even deeper. You can't simply address *how* to stop procrastinating without wrestling honestly with *why* you keep putting things off. Procrastination has hidden causes that lurk in our hearts. I believe that nothing will help you discern the thoughts and intentions of your heart better than the Scriptures.[1] Through the Word, we can unmask those hidden causes. In both the Old and New Testaments, God uses images that help us tap our personal motives for procrastination. The unwise steward is fearful;[2] the overconfident optimist is prideful;[3] and the poor planner is lazy.[4] While each may differ in their motivation, they bring the same result: *put off until tomorrow what could be done today.*

In the Bible, we discover God's thoughts on procrastination. Through Jesus' example, we learn how he was victorious over procrastination's subtle temptations, and as we walk in the Spirit we can develop new habits that will keep us from putting off until tomorrow what we should have done today. So don't put it off any longer. The mountain doesn't get any smaller because you wait until tomorrow to climb it. If it feels like you're running out of time, start taking it back today.

THINK LIKE GOD THINKS
Fear: The Secret Motivator

PROCRASTINATION is a manmade defense in response to fear. Perhaps you haven't stated it that boldly yet, but whether you're putting off a difficult project or a potential confrontation, there's a good chance you're afraid. Jesus reveals this truth when he tells the story of the three stewards.[5] A *steward* is one who is given charge over certain assets by his master.[6] He is not the owner of those assets, nor has he earned them.[7] In the story, each steward was given responsibility for a sum of money that they were to invest wisely. In Jesus' parable each steward was entrusted with certain talents by their master. The word *talent* describes the value of the assets with which they were entrusted. The three stewards were given 5 talents, 3 talents, and 1 talent respectively. In biblical language, a talent was a financial measurement and could be valued in silver or gold. A talent of silver was worth approximately $384,000 in modern US dollars; a talent of gold about $5,760,000.[8] By the gold standard, the first was entrusted with 29 million dollars, the second 17 million dollars, and the third 5.75 million dollars. That's a lot of somebody else's money to be responsible for.

Stewards one and two invested the money wisely, doubled their investment, and fulfilled their master's expectations. The master commended them for a job well done.[9] But the third steward chose not to invest the talent. As hard as it is to believe, he took a shovel, walked into his back yard, dropped nearly six million dollars into a hole in the ground, and covered it up. He then returned to his home and waited for the master's return. Don't you want to jump into Jesus' story, grab the unwise steward by the shoulders, shake him and shout, "What are you thinking?! How can you bury six million dollars in your back yard?" But upon the master's return, the one-talent steward told us what he was thinking. As we listen in, we will discover the hidden motivator behind our own struggle with procrastination. Here was his confession: *Master, I knew you to be a hard man, reaping where you did not sow, and gathering where you scattered no seed, so I was afraid, and I went and hid your talent in the ground. Here you have what is yours.*[10]

With three words he made his case for procrastinating: *I was afraid.* Throughout the Bible, self-confessed fear is often the cause of inaction or the wrong kind of action. Consider these examples:

- When Adam sinned in the Garden of Eden, he should have sought out God for a solution, but he sought a place to hide instead. When discovered, he responded: *I was afraid.*[11]

- When Jacob questioned his father-in-law's intentions, he should have addressed him, but he chose to run under the protection of night instead. When captured, he responded: *I was afraid.*[12]

- When Elihu, the youngest of Job's counselors was intimidated by the age of the other three, he sat in silence, and later confessed: *I was afraid.*[13]

- When the prophet Daniel was overwhelmed by the appearance of the archangel Gabriel, he fell on his face. Later he claimed: *I was afraid.*[14]

Fear can be debilitating. It can freeze your thoughts, lock down your emotions, and paralyze your ability to choose.

When it comes to procrastination, there are two elements in our fear that prevail—a sense of our inadequacy and the memory of past failed attempts.[15]

A Sense of Inadequacy

This is too difficult. If you put it off, it will get easier.

When we put off today's trouble because we feel inadequate, we often discover that the situation only becomes more difficult, not easier. The unwise steward claimed he was inadequate for the task. He believed his master's standard was too high for his ability. Succumbing to fear, he put off his responsibility as a steward to invest the money.[16] When we read the story, it is easy to empathize with the one-talent steward. We understand his fear. If we were entrusted with six million dollars, we'd feel inadequate too!

As a counselor, I've noticed often that when people are facing a task for which they feel inadequate, well-intentioned friends are prone to tell them that they can do it—they simply need to believe in themselves. These words, while meant for encouragement, can actually be quite dangerous. The Bible teaches that when you feel inadequate in your own strength or ability, it may actually be justified. Proverbs says,

> Trust in the LORD with all your heart, and *do not lean on your own understanding.* In all your ways acknowledge him, and he will make straight your paths" [emphasis added].[17]

When you do not feel up to the task to which God has called you, it should motivate you to trust in him more than you do in yourself. This is how you overcome your sense of inadequacy. When Gideon was afraid, he was assured that the Lord would fight for him.[18] The same is true of David who declared that Goliath wasn't fighting against a shepherd boy, but against the Lord.[19] Imagine if the one-talent steward had taken this approach. While he may have felt personally inadequate for the task, his confidence should have been in his master's prudent choice of him. The master who had acquired millions of dollars should have been wise enough to size up the stewards he chose to use. That's why we read that the master gave to each steward "according to his ability."[20] The master knew best. But the steward trusted in his perception of himself more than the master's estimation of his abilities. Hence, he grew afraid. Likewise, our Master has perfect wisdom. He knows all things actual and possible and what is best for us. When God brought the people of Israel out of Egypt, circa 1490 BC, the shortest route to the promised land would have been Northeast along the Mediterranean Sea. The road was known as the Way of the Philistines. But the shortest path was not the way God chose for them. In his wisdom, he took them through the wilderness to the edge of the Red Sea.[21] The Scripture records,

> When Pharaoh let the people go, God did not lead them by way of the land of the Philistines, although that was near. For God said, "Lest the people change their minds when they see war and return to Egypt." But God led the people around by the way of the wilderness toward the Red Sea. And the people of Israel went up out of the land of Egypt equipped for battle.[22]

If the people of Israel were equipped for battle, and they had the Lord of heaven's armies on their side, why not take the most direct route? Because an all-wise God knew that they would be afraid. This is what theologian Wayne

Grudem means when he says that God's knowledge is so complete that he knows possibilities as if they were realities.[23] When we fear what lies ahead and sense our own inadequacy, we would do well to remember what the one-talent steward did not: our Master prepared the events and opportunities before us according to our ability. To overcome the fear of inadequacy, we don't need to grow more confident in our own ability, but in God's wisdom, power, and loving choice of us.[24] Our confidence must grow in the wisdom of God, not in our ability or aptitude.

Finally, when we put something off, it doesn't get easier. Perhaps this principle is most often realized in our broken relationships. When we put off a conversation that we need to have with a friend or family member, we only weaken our appeal that we genuinely care about them. Furthermore, as days turn into weeks and weeks turn into years, we lose our motivation to do what we should have done all along. If Jesus had spoken in our vernacular, he might have said, "Just pick up the phone and do it. Deal with today's troubles today, and trust the Father with tomorrow."

A memory of a past failure

Since you failed before, you will only fail again. Don't try today.

Your past may be haunted with disappointments; personal failures may clutter your memory. Wherever there were breakdowns in your past, you'll find it easy to procrastinate in your present. Your thoughts whisper: *if you've failed before, you'll only fail again.* Our fear of repeated failure has barred the door to change. We wait for a motivation that never comes.

Perhaps you have struggled in your past with maintaining a weight-loss program. You were motivated when you started and you saw some early success, but then you failed to keep up the regime. The weight came back on, discouragement crept in, and now you've lost the motivation to begin again. You don't remember the brief successes, you just remember the feeling of failure. Better to put a smile on it, and act like it doesn't bother you. You put off the notorious "first day" until tomorrow. After that, you put it off further, always looking for the motivation that never comes. To rediscover the motivation necessary to crawl back on the treadmill, you will need to address the fear of repeated failure.

The Bible says that "perfect love casts out fear."[25] I have always been fascinated by that verse. You would think that perfect courage, endurance, or bravery might be one of the best candidates to cast out fear, but the Holy Spirit chose perfect love.[26] Our heavenly Father's perfect love is best understood through the sacrifice of Jesus in our place.[27] For the Bible says, "God shows his love for us in that while we were still sinners, Christ died for us."[28] Often, because of past failures, a person is afraid to try. They aren't motivated by "perfect love," they are motivated by their own perfection. They refuse to try again unless they are guaranteed success. But whenever we worry about personal success our pride is at work.[29] We don't simply fear failure, we fear the humbling process that comes with it. It's easier to say, "I'm going to start a weight loss program tomorrow" than to say, "I started one yesterday, but I couldn't keep it up." The first position is easier, because it doesn't acknowledge our personal weakness. We admire humility in others, but we dislike the failure that brings it about in us. Failure forces us to admit that we lack the strength to accomplish our goals. Our pride is like an angry pit bull—aggressive, defensive, and never looking for help from others. This latter position, "I started a weight-loss program yesterday but couldn't keep it up," forces you to ask for help from God and from others.

If we will let personal failure accomplish its intended purpose, it will humble us, and we'll ask for help next time.[30] We won't attempt to operate in our own wisdom; we'll ask God for his.[31] We'll trust in him, not ourselves.[32] This is the value of personal failure, and you can be certain that the devil and all of his angels don't want you discovering it. They whisper the lie: *Don't ask for help. Just put this off until you have the strength of will to do it on your own.*

Consider this: if you start today, what's the worst thing that can happen? You fail, humble yourself, try again, and become a little bit more like Jesus in the process.[33] But so often our nagging fear of failure prompts us to put off the things we've messed up in the past. Our fear of failure is really fruitless because it doesn't encourage planning; it offers unproductive waiting instead. The longer we put off the task we've failed at before, the harder it is to get started. We need to admit that we are weak and insecure. Left to our own, we would fail again. Such an understanding allows you to take a step forward by faith. You will never discover the motivation you lack by waiting to start. The one who is growing in faith acknowledges his past failures and trusts God with future endeavors. You go forward with a confidence in God's perfect love, not your past achievements.[34]

There is an irony to the parable of the one-talent steward. While the steward was afraid of failing, his master wasn't afraid of giving him the chance to try. Even if the steward's fears told him otherwise, he should have placed his confidence in the truth that his master knew best and had actually taken his abilities into consideration. The master had tailored each opportunity with such discernment in view: "To one he gave five talents, to another two, to another one, *to each according to his ability*" [emphasis added].[35] The fact that the others had more talents should have strengthened the steward's confidence in his master's wisdom. More was not expected of him than he could deliver. The greater talents given the other two stewards should have confirmed this realization, but fear took over. The thought of failure caused him to falter; perhaps tomorrow would provide a better opportunity. But tomorrow only brought less time until the master's return, and now his investment would need to pay a greater return, requiring great risk. Fear swept in again: *Rather than make a mistake, wait and see what the next day holds*, it whispered. Eventually, fear caused the steward to question his master's wisdom. *What was he thinking when he gave me this much money? This is too much for me to handle. If I do try to invest it, I'm sure to lose it. Better to sit tight.*

The unwise steward teaches us a significant truth about fear and procrastination. Because God never gives you more than you can handle, when you procrastinate because of fear, you are doubting the wisdom of The Master—just like the unwise steward.[36]

At first reading, it appears that the unwise steward blamed his fear on his master. He replied, "Master I knew you to be a hard man . . . so I was afraid."[37] But the confident assertion, "I knew you" can also be understood as "I perceived you."[38] This is a subtle shift, but an important one. Perceptions are tricky things. They stoke fear's fire, and they do so regardless of their truthfulness. With the phrases, "reaping where you did not sow" and "gathering where you scattered no seed,"[39] the steward paints a picture of the master that sounds more like a pirate than a protector. In his mind, he views his master as a ruthless opportunist—like a loan shark trolling the most impoverished communities. Yet, nowhere in the rest of the story is this position justified.[40] The master is simply referred to as "a man going on a journey." And the two faithful servants do not share this perspective. They are invited to "enter into the joy of the master."[41] This is why perceptions are dangerous. Our perceptions are convincing even if they are not grounded in truth.[42] Our fear grows as we spend time thinking on these false perceptions; we become even more certain they are true. Not only do our perceptions feed our fears, but our fears seem to shape and build our perceptions, making us even more confident of their accuracy. But we must remember that they are simply our perceptions.

The unwise steward falsely reasoned that if his master would take from people who didn't owe him anything, he would certainly expect something unreasonable from him as a steward. The order in the parable worked like this: *a false perception generated a paralyzing fear with procrastination as the end result.* This is why you can't fix the procrastination problem simply with time management tools. Fear of a circumstance or individual is lurking below the surface of your tendency to procrastinate.[43] That fear is driving your decision to put off until tomorrow what you could have done today.

Franklin D. Roosevelt became President of the United States with his country in the grips of the great depression. At his inauguration address, he delivered one of the lines for which he is famous: "Let me assert my firm belief that the only thing we have to fear is...fear itself." He went on to define fear as the "nameless, unreasoning, unjustified terror which paralyzes." A little known fact about FDR is that he took his oath of office using a family Bible that was published in 1686, the oldest Bible ever used in an inaugural ceremony. Roosevelt requested that the Bible be opened to 1 Corinthians 13.[44] There we read:

> Love is patient and kind; love does not envy or boast; it is not arrogant or rude. It does not insist on its own way; it is not irritable or resentful; it does not rejoice at wrongdoing, but rejoices with the truth. Love bears all things, believes all things, hopes all things, endures all things. Love never ends.[45]

While he never referenced this truth in his speech, FDR had placed his hand on God's solution for overcoming debilitating fear. The Bible teaches that perfect love casts out fear,[46] and God's love is perfect love.[47]

Pride: The Overconfident Optimist

MY DENTIST warned me, but I didn't listen. "A temporary crown," he said, "is only temporary. Make an appointment to see me in about 30 days; by that time your permanent crown will be ready and we'll make sure we protect that root canal." I scheduled my next visit, but a severe storm closed the office the day of the appointment. They called and left several messages, but when you've developed the habit of procrastination, it's pretty easy to not return a call from the dentist. Life got busy, and I forgot his warning. Months passed—18 to be exact. When I finally scheduled the appointment, the news wasn't good. "A temporary crown can't protect the tooth from decay, like a permanent one can. Decay has begun, and the situation has been compromised. I can do my best to attach the permanent crown, but at some point this tooth will need to be extracted." I must have looked confused because he added, "The reason you didn't feel the effects of the decay, was that we removed the nerve when we did the root canal." While my dentist felt bad, it wasn't his fault. My tendency to procrastinate made me responsible. I should have known better.

American investor and author of *Rich Dad, Poor Dad*, Robert Kiyosaki reminds us, "Your future is determined by what you do today, not tomorrow."[48] The procrastinator gets comfortable believing that tomorrow will provide a better opportunity than today. Then, when tomorrow actually comes, it's that much easier to wait for the day that follows. Banking on the idea that tomorrow will provide a better opportunity than today reveals our overconfidence. Benjamin Franklin said, "Work while it is called today, for you know not how much you may be hindered tomorrow. One today is worth two tomorrows; never leave that till tomorrow which you can do today."[49]

Tomorrow rarely provides the opportunities that today does. Jesus said that tomorrow would have troubles all its own.[50] The lesson I learned in the dentist's chair that day was: *While I had chosen to wait, decay had not.* It had begun its silent work the moment I had left the office 18 months earlier. What's true in the dentist's chair is true in your marriage, church, and community. You may wait, but decay goes to work right away. When you procrastinate, you don't immediately feel the consequences of putting off what should be done. It's like a deadened nerve in your tooth. The student that doesn't turn in an assignment or two doesn't feel the effects until mid-term grades come out. The nagging pain in his chest doesn't send the man in his mid-life to the doctor until the heart attack comes. The effects of extra helpings of dessert don't show up the next morning, they show up the next month.

This gradual decay affects our relationships as well. Jesus said, "If your brother sins against you, go and tell him his fault, between you and him alone. If he listens to you, you have gained your brother."[51] Jesus chose the present tense for *go*, not the future tense. He's saying *go* immediately. Don't put it off. There's a chance you can gain your brother, but that chance decreases exponentially when you wait.

Since communication is the number one reason given for most divorces, there's a good chance that procrastination has killed more marriages than adultery. The initial conflict, no matter how sticky, is easier to resolve before bitterness has settled in. We find a similar warning in Ephesians: "Do not let the sun go down on your anger, and give no opportunity to the devil."[52] Eugene Peterson translates that phrase, "Don't give the Devil that kind of foothold in your life."[53] In the context of broken communication, procrastination gives Satan an opportunity he otherwise wouldn't have. Make no mistake about it, he knows how to exploit it.

When my grandmother died, my parents passed her Bible on to me. When I opened it, a small piece of paper fell out. I recognized the handwriting as my grandmother's. I'd certainly received my share of warnings from her growing up with her right down the street. But this time it was like she was giving one last warning from beyond the grave. The note read: *Beware the fire storm. Any trouble you put off until tomorrow will quickly become far worse. Deal with it today.* How I wish I had heeded her advice. But I've failed to do so enough times that I know firsthand the truth of that warning.

The idea that tomorrow will be better than today is pride's subtle lie. Frankly, you don't even know that you have tomorrow, but you do have today. Humility works today and doesn't make assumptions about tomorrow. James gave this word of warning:

> Come now, you who say, "Today or tomorrow we will go into such and such a town and spend a year there and trade and make a profit"—yet you do not know what tomorrow will bring. What is your life? For you are a mist that appears for a little time and then vanishes. Instead you ought to say, "If the Lord wills, we will live and do this or that." As it is, you boast in your arrogance.[54]

While this passage appears to be describing an overconfident businessman, try viewing it through the lens of a procrastinator. Both the self-assured businessman and the tentative procrastinator have this in common: they are banking on the fact that they have tomorrow. While it may be more subtle on the part of the procrastinator, there is presumption in that thought. His problem is not time; his problem is pride. Until he humbles himself regarding his overconfident optimism, he will continue to put off until tomorrow what he could have done today. But in truth, we don't know what tomorrow holds, so we should make a humble investment in tomorrow by being diligent today.

The overconfident optimist sees today and tomorrow as the same.

Today *or* tomorrow. It's a small difference, but it communicates a great deal about the procrastinator's thought process. He does not say today *and* tomorrow—meaning he needs both days to get the work done. He does not say today *instead of* tomorrow—meaning he believes all the work can be done today. He says today *or* tomorrow, meaning he sees both days as legitimate options. You could take the "or" out of the sentence and put in an equal sign. The procrastinator sees the two days as the same, but they are not. James is giving a warning: *You know you have today, you should not be so confident about tomorrow.* Only God knows the future with certainty. In Jeremiah we read: "'For I know the plans I have for you' declares the Lord"[55] We can plan. We can guess. We can imagine. But only God *knows*.

If you knew you only had one week left on earth would you spend it differently than you were planning? What things have you been putting off that you would attempt to complete? Perhaps a broken relationship, an unfulfilled promise, or a commitment that you've yet to meet? One of the best things that a procrastinator can do is live as if there's no tomorrow. That doesn't mean that he tries to jam more into a 24-hour day, it means that he doesn't make assumptions that he has tomorrow when he may not. At the end of the day, he humbly gives God thanks for the day that he was given, and he prayerfully trusts God with tomorrow. He doesn't assume that it will be there.

The overconfident optimist envisions more time than he actually has.

Note that the overconfident optimist is planning on spending "a year there" when he finally gets to his destination. During that year, he's planning on "making a profit." First, he assumed that *today* and *tomorrow* were the same. Now he has assumed that the next 365 days will have equal opportunity as well. There's an old English proverb that says "What can be done at any time is never done at all." James reminds the overconfident that his life is like a vapor. It's going to dissipate far more quickly than anticipated. This is a really important image for the prideful procrastinator. He will always assume he has more time than he really has. But projects take longer than expected.[56] Rebuilding broken relationships won't happen overnight.[57] The Scripture says that our life is only "a mist" that exists for a "little time." Life is like a vapor—it's here today and gone tomorrow.

When I would get sick as a child, my mom would pull the vaporizer out of the closet, fill it with water, and place it next to my bed. I can still remember the distinct odor of the steam as it would rise up next to my pillow, easing my cough and clearing my congestion. As long as the unit was plugged in the mist appeared, but the moment it was unplugged the mist was gone. Sure, it might have hung in the air for a second or two, but then it disappeared into thin air, just as if it had never existed. When friends of mine began publishing their music together, they considered calling themselves *The Vapors*. They based the idea on this verse in James, and they were fond of saying, "We just want to make the most of our mist." The wife succumbed to lung cancer before her 40th birthday, but she left behind a legacy of songs she had written and recorded. Because both she and her husband desired to "make the most of their mist," we are left with her creativity to inspire us, and her sweet voice to listen to even after she's gone. She could have put off the desire to write the lyrics and melodies until a more convenient time, but she chose to view her life as a vapor instead. The one who learns to "number his days" will not live as if he has more time. He will learn to view time as short, and seek to steward it well.

The steward lives under the daily reality that his life is not his own. Both the businessman in the James passage and the procrastinator forget this truth. The businessman doesn't consult God about his plans for tomorrow, and the procrastinator doesn't check with God before he moves today's plans to tomorrow. Both have forgotten they are stewards. God is not consulted by the procrastinator until the procrastinator is in a panic. Only then does he call out for help because he realizes he can't get it all done in the time remaining. Remarkably, if the procrastinator saw his time as if he were a steward and not the owner, most of his problems would go away. He would ask God's permission before pushing a task off until the next day. He would submit to the Spirit's direction through the Scriptures. He would follow Jesus' example to accomplish things in a timely manner.[58] This is why I refer to the procrastinator as the "arrogant optimist." He takes his stewardship of time far too lightly. He assumes it's his own. He doesn't seek counsel from others or from God regarding how to spend it. He spends today's time on what he deems best, and pushes off the unfinished tasks for tomorrow. His attitude will need to change or his procrastinating habits never will.

Laziness: The Stubborn Enabler

A WILD SLOTH can sleep 15-18 hours a day, which is about as much as a domestic house cat. Most procrastinators I know would prefer not to be compared to a sloth. They might work 15-18 hours a day, but they wouldn't consider sleeping that much (even if they'd like to). They pride themselves in long hours spent at the office, sacrificing vacations, getting up early, and staying up late. But while the Bible instructs us to avoid laziness,[59] it also warns us to not think too highly of ourselves.[60] In other words, we're all prone to laziness—it may just be hiding where we least expect it. The hardworking employee may struggle to put in that same effort with his family. Perhaps a dad procrastinates on the hard work of developing a relationship around his son's interests until it's too late. Or a wife may give hours to developing ministry opportunities with other women, but might find conversations with her husband to be difficult and burdensome. Pride tells us we're working hard when, in truth, we may only be working hard at the things that come easy to us or that we enjoy.

While the sloth describes our temptation to put things off, the Bible presents another animal to consider when overcoming a lazy spirit: the ant. In contrast to the sloth, the ant sleeps less than five hours a day. Debby Cassill and a team of colleagues at the University of South Florida in St. Petersburg recently verified this.

> Worker [ants] fell asleep at irregular intervals, and not at the same time. But the sheer number of incredibly short naps they took was striking. On average, a single worker ant would take 250 naps each day, with each

one lasting just over a minute. That equates to 4 hours and 48 minutes of sleep a day.[61]

But it isn't just the ant's work ethic that God holds up as a pattern for us. It's her instinctive tendency to do her work ahead of time. She "prepares" herself months before the need arises, and she gathers her food while there is still time to spare. God commends the ant for the fact that she doesn't procrastinate—she prepares. Read the Proverb carefully.

> Go to the ant, O sluggard; consider her ways, and be wise. Without having any chief, officer, or ruler, she *prepares* her bread in summer and *gathers* her food in harvest. How long will you lie there, O sluggard? When will you arise from your sleep?[62] [emphasis added]

We are to consider the ant's *ways*. The word *ways* is sometimes used to mean a path, roadway, or journey. But it can also mean a manner of life.[63] God wants us to look at the ant's journey. She foregoes sleep because she's getting ready for the future. She doesn't *wait* for tomorrow; she *prepares* for it.[64]

The focus on preparation is helpful for the procrastinator. Even hard workers can struggle with laziness when it comes to doing what they don't want to do. It's easy to blame our circumstances when all the while we have misused the time God has provided—like the student who tries to print their paper at the very last minute only to discover a computer glitch. They may blame the hardware, but if they had started the project (and completed it) earlier, they would have had sufficient time to deal with the technological hiccup. The lesson to be learned from the ant is not simply to develop a strong work ethic, but also to plan ahead.

For procrastinators, the tendency towards laziness will most often be revealed when there appears to be an abundance of time. Most procrastinators are motivated to work when they can envision short time limits like the end of the day or work week. But they struggle when the time frame is so far in advance that it seems indefinite, like the end of the semester or retirement. In these instances, the procrastinator will usually put short term pleasure ahead of long term planning. He will ignore the counsel of the ant who prepared her bread in summer (while there was still time), and he will be unprepared for winter when it arrives. Because ants are coldblooded they enter into a groggy hibernation state during the winter, being only a few inches under the ground. But there is a species of ants known as the *Messor Aciculatus* that actually carry plant seeds into their nests and store them there. Then, during winter, they feed on the stored seeds. Without their pre-planning, they would starve to death and lose the entire colony by spring.

The Old Testament character of Joseph reveals three simple steps for overcoming the difficulty of time management that plagues the procrastinator. The earlier part of Joseph's life had been challenging; he'd been sold in to slavery by his brothers,[65] falsely accused, and thrown into prison.[66] Then, having correctly interpreted the dreams of two prisoners, he was forgotten by one for an additional two years.[67] At this point, Pharaoh, King of Egypt, has a troublesome dream and Joseph is called forth to interpret it. Joseph not only interprets the dream properly, he also lays out a plan of preparation that marks him out as one in whom the Spirit of God resides.[68] Notice Joseph's words:

> It is as I told Pharaoh; God has shown to Pharaoh what he is about to do. There will come seven years of

great plenty throughout all the land of Egypt, but after them there will arise seven years of famine, and all the plenty will be forgotten in the land of Egypt. The famine will consume the land, and the plenty will be unknown in the land by reason of the famine that will follow, for it will be very severe. And the doubling of Pharaoh's dream means that the thing is fixed by God, and God will shortly bring it about. Now therefore let Pharaoh select a discerning and wise man, and set him over the land of Egypt.[69]

(1) The procrastinator must remember that God is sovereign over time, but he himself is not.

The Psalmist writes, "From everlasting to everlasting you are God."[70] God is eternal, unlimited by time. But our lives are lived within the intrinsic limitations of the space-time continuum. Joseph made it clear to Pharaoh that God was the one in charge of the upcoming 14 years, that the *thing was fixed by God*, revealed as an expression of his sovereign grace. Such a statement would have come as a surprise to Pharaoh, as most of the Egyptian kings saw themselves as deities. Yet, here was the true and living God informing the self-proclaimed god (Pharaoh) how he should spend his time for the next 14 years. Most of us see ourselves as sovereign over time, not stewards of it. Both the homeless man walking the streets of New York City and the Manhattan CEO hurriedly passing him by believe that they have the right to use their time as they wish. We may not be in control of much, we reason, but at least we should be in charge of how we spend our time. But Joseph had spent 13 years learning what it means to be a steward;[71] he had learned that opportunities were provided by God and therefore ought not to be squandered on himself. Even in the darkness of an Egyptian prison he had used his time to focus on others[72] and give glory to God.[73] Throughout his troubled life, he had grown in both of these areas, so he was prepared for the moment.[74]

(2) The procrastinator must see time as an opportunity to prepare for the future, not simply to indulge in today's pleasures.

While God would send seven years of famine, he would first send seven years of plenty. Like the ant in Proverbs, Joseph saw the seven years of plenty as the time to prepare. Remember, the procrastinator usually chooses short-term pleasure over long-term planning. The procrastinator sees the seven years of plenty not as an opportunity to prepare, but as an opportunity to eat, drink and be merry. This is what prompted Victor Kiam, CEO of Remington to fire off: "Procrastination is opportunity's natural assassin."[75] The college student spends the early part of the semester gaming, partying, or binging on movies rather than getting started on the year-end projects. The father puts off his eight-year-old daughter's soccer game, figuring he has plenty of games to watch later. The borderline diabetic disregards dietary changes until his condition is full-blown. When we believe we have plenty of time, we put off what is truly important. Herein lies the arrogance of the procrastinator's optimism: it is prideful to believe tomorrow will offer the same opportunity that you have today. It is arrogant to presume upon a future that only God, in his wisdom, knows.[76] The early days of a student's semester, for instance, are best spent planning for the closing days of the semester. But the end seems so far off, and the week-ends so inviting, that he puts off his responsibilities. The father assumes his daughter will always have the same exuberance for him to cheer as she does as an eight-year old. Both the college student and the father have something in common: they don't see time as an opportunity to prepare for the future. The temptation to put it off happens easily when time seems plentiful; it's only later, when we've run out of time, that we feel the urgency and attempt to make it up.

(3) The procrastinator must develop a useful plan for whatever time remains.

Joseph became second in charge of the nation because he was the only one with a plan. His plan was simple: prepare for the future. He had been out of prison only 24 hours, yet he addressed the King of Egypt with clarity and boldness.

> Let Pharaoh proceed to appoint overseers over the land and take one-fifth of the produce of the land of Egypt during the seven plentiful years. And let them gather all the food of these good years that are coming and store up grain under the authority of Pharaoh for food in the cities, and let them keep it. That food shall be a reserve for the land against the seven years of famine that are to occur in the land of Egypt, so that the land may not perish through the famine.[77]

The seven years were so plentiful, that had any of the other Egyptians done what Joseph instructed Pharaoh to do—save up for the years of famine—they would have been fine. But they didn't use the years of plenty to prepare for the years of famine. Without a plan, and without embracing it early, they were unprepared when the difficult time came.

They were completely dependent upon Pharaoh's benevolence, and they became his slaves.[78] This is about as real as a picture can get. When you begin your work in advance of the due date, you have the freedom to choose how you spend your time. But if you squander that time, as you near the due date, you not only have less time, you also have less freedom. You have fewer options for how you will spend your time. Procrastinators live by the adage, "Nothing in the world is so urgent that it couldn't become even more urgent tomorrow." As your level of urgency increases, your freedom of choice decreases.

(4) The procrastinator must understand that there are unavoidable consequences if he doesn't prepare in advance.

In Joseph's final plea with Pharaoh he says, "And the doubling of Pharaoh's dream means that the thing is fixed by God, and God will shortly bring it about."[79] In other words, the famine was coming whether or not Pharaoh made preparations. There was no changing it, and it was coming swiftly. Most procrastinators foolishly believe that they can avoid the consequences of not preparing in advance. They are convinced that somehow they will be the exception to the rule, but sadly they are not. Their moment of reckoning comes, ready or not.

One of my favorite stories as a child was Aesop's fable of the grasshopper and the ant. With a Proverbs-like commitment, the ant worked hard all summer, preparing for the winter while the grasshopper danced a jig with his fiddle and sang his summer away. The unavoidable consequence of winter came, and the ant was prepared, but the grasshopper was not. The window of opportunity had closed for harvest; the ground was frozen, blanketed in white. The ant told the grasshopper to go "dance upon the snow." Needless to say, it was a very brief jig.

I've met some very busy procrastinators. They don't appear to be lazy on the surface. But when you are always doing things at the last minute, you are not diligent in your preparation. You are lazy in your planning. You need to heed the lesson of the ant, lest you go the way of the grasshopper.

DO WHAT JESUS DID

IF THERE was ever a time that Jesus might have succumbed to the kind of fear that reveals itself in procrastination, it would have been his impending crucifixion. The Scripture teaches that the very thought of being on the cross and incurring the wrath of the Father terrorized Jesus.[80] Yet, in reference to his crucifixion Luke records, "When the days drew near for him to be taken up, he set his face to go to Jerusalem."[81] His ministry in Galilee had been prolific. He was still admired by many. His adversaries, the religious leaders, controlled Jerusalem and were intent on taking his life. A return to Jerusalem at this stage in his ministry had only one purpose: the cross and mankind's salvation.[82]

Nevertheless, with soldier-like resolve he *set his face*. He didn't procrastinate on the hard things. He didn't allow fear to move him away from the will of God. Robert Stein comments, "Knowing the divine plan, Jesus (literally) 'set his face to go to Jerusalem' in order to fulfill God's purpose for his life. He was determined to follow God's plan and deliberately initiated the precipitating events."[83] John Piper reminds us that to move towards Jerusalem was to move away from certain wishes or desires.

> Remember, when you think of Jesus' resolution to die, that he had a nature like ours. He shrunk back from pain like we do. He would have enjoyed marriage and children and grandchildren and a long life and esteem in the community. He had a mother and brothers and sisters. He had special places in the mountains. To turn his back on all this and set his face towards vicious whipping and beating and spitting and mocking and crucifixion was not easy. It was hard.[84]

The cross is the kind of thing that would have motivated a weaker man to procrastinate while he looked for another way out. Jesus himself requested another way from his Father on the eve of his crucifixion in the Garden of Gethsemane,[85] but it was in the context of not waiting or pushing back the date. For the months that led up to that moment, he had been resolute in moving towards Jerusalem and the cross that awaited him.[86] On that very difficult journey, the Gospels reveal help for those of us who are tempted to put off the hard things for a more convenient time.

(1) Rely on the Word

To avoid putting off the hardest of tasks, Jesus made choices in light of what he knew he was supposed to do from the Word of God. Luke 18:31 reminds us,

> And taking the twelve, he said to them, "See, we are going up to Jerusalem, and everything that is *written about the Son of Man by the prophets* will be accomplished. For he will be delivered over to the Gentiles and will be mocked and shamefully treated and spit upon. And after flogging him, they will kill him, and on the third day he will rise. But they understood none of these things [emphasis added].[87]

Jesus' words seem so straight-forward that it's hard to imagine how the disciples didn't get it. Perhaps it was the popularity of his ministry that made them unable to see how quickly the multitude would turn on him. In fact, on other occasions where Jesus spoke of his crucifixion they tried to talk him out of it.[88] But Jesus wasn't looking for their affirmation. He didn't need their approval. He spoke to them about what he had discovered about his mission in

Old Testament Prophecies. Perhaps he had in mind Psalm 22 or 69, Isaiah 53, or Zechariah 13:7.[89] Jesus had found the will of God in the Word of God and he was intent upon completing the task. The same should be true of us. To overcome procrastination, find a Biblical passage that directs you in the will of God and cling to it. The biblical passage will not only inform your decision, it will lend conviction when you feel like procrastinating. When you are tempted to put off a difficult conversation or task, *rehearse the verse* and take your first step by faith.[90]

(2) Recite your purpose

As we've already discussed, fear is the hidden motivator behind procrastination. Perhaps you're afraid of a project you don't know how to accomplish or a conversation with a person you assume will go poorly. Maybe you know you need to exercise, but are afraid of the discouragement that will come if you lack the physical stamina to keep it up. So you put it off until a more convenient time, but that time never comes; tomorrow never arrives. As the 19th century poet Charles Baudelaire said, "In putting off what one has to do, one runs the risk of never being able to do it."[91] In the final week of his earthly life, Jesus was deeply troubled by the cross. Notice his words:

> Now is my soul troubled. And what shall I say? "Father, save me from this hour?" But *for this purpose I have come to this hour* [emphasis added].[92]

Though fearful, Jesus doesn't surrender to that fear; instead, he recites his purpose, his cause for coming to earth. A few verses later, in John's gospel, Jesus adds, "And I, when I am lifted up from the earth, will draw all people to myself." John adds this commentary: "He said this to show by what kind of death he was going to die." [93]

Not only did Jesus recite his purpose, but he clarified that he wasn't simply doing this for himself. His intention was to bring glory to God. "Father" he said, "glorify your name."[94] Jesus teaches us a vital lesson. When we view ourselves as the center, it's easy for fear to grow, and as fear grows so does our tendency to procrastinate. Jesus made the glory of the Father central to his purpose; in doing so, his attention was off of himself and it was easier for him to make the ultimate sacrifice. Furthermore, he maintained the attitude of a servant, and he encouraged us to do the same. Mark recounts him having said, "But whoever would be great among you must be your servant, and whoever would be first among you must be slave of all. For even the Son of Man came not to be served but to serve, and to give his life as a ransom for many."[95] As opposed to putting off the most difficult task of his life, Jesus recited the purpose for which he came, kept the glory of God central, and maintained the attitude of a servant. In so doing, he was able to reestablish the courage necessary to move forward.

(3) Rest in the Father

The phrase *Jesus set his face towards Jerusalem* harkens back to a passage in Isaiah 50:7. There we read:

> But the Lord GOD helps me; therefore I have not been disgraced; therefore I have *set my face like a flint*, and I know that I shall not be put to shame [emphasis added].

A flint is a hard, dark piece of quartz. When struck with steel it would cast a spark, but because of its hardness it would not be destroyed. It's the perfect picture of an unwavering resolve. But this resolve is not some internal, man

-made commitment. Rather, it finds it source in the opening phrase of the verse: *But the Lord God helps me.* It is what allows us to trust in the Father's help as we take on the difficult task. *The MacArthur Study Bible* adds this note of interpretation,

> So sure was he of the Lord God's help that he resolutely determined to remain unswayed by whatever hardship might await Him.[96]

Jesus' confidence was in his Father. He was confident that God would help him in his hour of need, and he encouraged us to do the same.

In the Old Testament, King David faced a lion, a bear, and the giant enemy, Goliath. In each of those battles his confidence was in God, not himself. In Psalm 37, he lays out this focus in four phrases: trust in the Lord, delight yourself in the Lord, commit your way to the Lord, and be still before the Lord.[97] Those phrases become excellent patterns for prayer as we practice a dependence on the Lord God. (For a prayer pattern developed around these phrases see *Safe in the Storm: biblical strategies for overcoming anxiety*, 61).

(4) Reach for Eternity

On the night before Jesus died, he informed his disciples that he would shortly be leaving.

> In my Father's house are many rooms. If it were not so, would I have told you that I go to prepare a place for you? And if I go and prepare a place for you, I will come again and will take you to myself, that where I am you may be also.[98]

Two times in this passage the word "prepare" occurs in the context of eternity. Remember, preparing in advance is a major challenge for the procrastinator. Simply apply that truth to the scope of your entire life, and you will understand what Jesus knew—you ought to be preparing for eternity.[99] The Bible encourages us to live with the recognition that this world is not all there is. C.S. Lewis believed that most Christians lived as if this world were their home and heaven was a far and distant land. He challenged his generation to reverse the metaphor. He said that we were living in the far country and heaven was our home. Imagine that you are an American Citizen, with a two-week vacation scheduled in Europe. Would you not attempt to do as much as you could in those 14 days, knowing that you would shortly be returning to your homeland? When we are reaching for eternity we won't procrastinate on the tasks that are before us because—in light of eternity—this life is so short-lived. Knowing that our citizenship is in heaven, should change the way that we spend our time on earth.

When I speak or serve in another part of the world, I often think that way. Sure, I enjoy the new sights and sounds of a distance land. I like to experience the culture and get to know its people. But by the end of the first week, I'm ready to go home. When I served on a humanitarian aid trip to Bosnia, I actually took out pictures of my wife and kids every night before I went to bed. I studied them, I remembered, and I smiled. I couldn't wait to see them again. After five days, I was homesick, but there were still seven days left of service. Those seven days were really productive days. We delivered medical supplies to a hospital, mattresses to widows in a village, and basic food supplies to refugees. Our team didn't procrastinate on any of these tasks. I didn't once think *I'll do this next week*, because the next week I was going home. Heaven isn't the far country—you're living in the far country. When you mistakenly call it home, you'll procrastinate on what should be done today. But when you set your eyes on heaven, you'll see today clearly, because you're hoping that tomorrow you'll be home.

LIVE BY THE SPIRIT

IT MIGHT surprise you to learn that one of the key passages on being filled with the Spirit[100] is proceeded by one of the most useful passages for overcoming procrastination. This is a reminder that our battle with procrastination is a spiritual one and that we must depend on the Holy Spirit if we hope to be victorious. In his letter to the Ephesians the apostle Paul records,

> Look carefully then how you walk, not as unwise but as wise, making the best use of the time, because the days are evil. Therefore do not be foolish, but understand what the will of the Lord is...and be filled with the Spirit.[101]

The various phrases in the Ephesians passage surface four essential questions regarding our use of time:

- Am I wasting time without realizing it?
- Am I investing time in what is truly important?
- Am I determining what is truly important from Biblical values?
- Am I applying self-control with the use of my time?

Four words will serve as a memory device as we answer these essential questions: (1) analyze, (2) prioritize, (3) biblicize, and (4) exercise. These words help us avoid the hazards that are hidden to most procrastinators. If we are willing to make changes to our daily lives in light of these discoveries we can be victorious over procrastination's stubborn tendencies.

(1) Analyze -- "look carefully how you walk"
Am I wasting time without realizing it?

Most procrastinators operate without personal accountability for their time. While they may admit to having not planned properly, they usually are unaware of how they spent their time. They only know they didn't seem to have enough of it. The phrase "look carefully then how you walk" challenges us to diligently evaluate our use of time. The word *carefully* is translated in other biblical passages as *closely, exactly, accurately*.[102] It brings to mind an analytical evaluation, one that focuses on the details, not the generalities. This is helpful counsel for procrastinators. They typically do not think of time in small increments (minutes and hours). They think in terms of days, weeks, or years. The procrastinator lives like someone who is constantly going into debt, because he assumes he'll make more money later. The compulsive shopper and procrastinator have a similar problem: they are frivolous with a God-given resource. For the spendthrift, it's about dollars; for the procrastinator, it's about minutes. The solution for both is to *look carefully how they walk*. They need to live by a budget. One needs to carefully plan how he'll spend his money; the other needs to carefully plan how he'll spend his time.

A few years ago, I found that I was growing increasingly discouraged with events in my life. Each week it felt like Friday came upon me too fast, leaving an ever-increasing mound of unfinished tasks. Those unfinished jobs cluttered my desk and my mind. I felt the emotional weariness that comes from falling further behind. I confessed my struggle to a friend and mentor.[103] He challenged me to keep a journal of my daily activities in 15 minute increments for two weeks. I remember thinking: *I don't have the time to do this! I can't complete my unfinished projects now and you want me to spend my time recording activities every 15 minutes?* But, out of respect for his wisdom I began the process. It was both humbling and revealing. After two weeks I began to see patterns in my life. I discovered areas where I was both unproductive and inefficient. I could also see where some of my relationships were not getting the time they needed, while others—because I hadn't planned properly—were getting an inordinate amount of time. Having not made priority-based decisions about my time, I was at the mercy of what others viewed as important. At the end of the journaling, I had to admit I was not making the best use of my time—a truth I would not have discovered if I had not taken the time to analyze. Heed the biblical warning: *look carefully how you walk* (see pages 68-69 for a sample 15-minute journal).

(2) Prioritize -- "making the best use of time"
Am I investing time in what is truly important?

The second phrase in the biblical passage, *making the best use of time*, speaks of priorities. Paul's not comparing *good* and *bad*, implying a moral decision. He's speaking of *better* and *best*, underscoring a priority-based decision. Some translations render this with the phrase, "redeeming the time." *Redeem* is a biblical word with a rich heritage. It literally means "buy for the purpose of setting free."[104] Purchasing time for the sake of freedom. Now that's good news for the procrastinator who is shackled by his many unfinished tasks. He needs to make better use of his time, and this is possible when he begins to make decisions in light of chosen priorities. The Bible often speaks of priorities.

Consider these two familiar passages:

- But seek first the kingdom of God and all these things will be added unto you.
- And this is the first commandment, you shall love the Lord your God with all your heart, soul, mind and strength.

One of the areas where laziness slips in for the procrastinator is in the setting of priorities. When we don't establish our priorities and make choices in light of them we will find that, often, decisions are made for us. Then, out of necessity, we will put off what is really important because the less important task has risen to the level of urgency. Jesus makes the same observation when he addresses Martha. She was doing the urgent task while neglecting the important.

> Now as they went on their way, Jesus entered a village. And a woman named Martha welcomed him into her house. And she had a sister called Mary, who sat at the Lord's feet and listened to his teaching. But Martha was distracted with much serving. And she went up to him and said, "Lord, do you not care that my sister has left me to serve alone? Tell her then to help me." But the Lord answered her, "Martha, Martha, you are anxious and troubled about many things, but one thing is necessary. Mary has chosen the good portion, which will not be taken away from her."[105]

R.H Stein comments,

> Martha also wanted to hear Jesus, but the tyranny of the urgent prevented her from doing this. Martha was too easily distracted by less important things. [...] There is a need to focus on what is most important, for although serving is good, sitting at Jesus' feet is best.[106]

Dwight D. Eisenhower served as the General of Armed

forces as well as President of the United States for two terms. Making the case for what is truly important, he is reported to have said,

> Especially whenever our affairs seem to be in crisis, we are almost compelled to give our first attention to the urgent present rather than to the important future.[107]

There is a thought-provoking matrix that bears Eisenhower's name.[108] The matrix has the support of numerous biblical passages,[109] and is helpful for evaluating our priorities in light of how we spend our time. The Eisenhower matrix comprises four quadrants. It is important to remember these boxes are never static. Picture the four boxes together as composing a 24-hour period. Then imagine that the individual boxes enlarge or contract based upon how you spend your time. In order for one to increase in size an accompanying box will need to decrease. As you attempt to determine priorities, the events of your day fall into one of these categories.

important AND urgent 1	important BUT not urgent 2
3 not important BUT urgent	4 not important AND not urgent

Quadrant 1 is the *important and urgent*. When the good Samaritan came upon the man who had been robbed and left for dead[110] it was both important (this is how we love our neighbor) *and* urgent (something needed to be done immediately).

Quadrant 2 is the *important but not urgent*. This is where preparation is done. The life of Jesus is an excellent example of this kind of activity. He prayed early in the morning on his busiest days,[111] learned the Scripture well in advance of temptation,[112] and always thoroughly prepared to teach and explain the Scriptures.[113] Your spiritual disciplines fall into quadrant 2. This is where the procrastinator spends the least amount of time because putting off quadrant 2 activities has no immediate consequence. This quadrant lacks urgency. The world will not come to an end if, for instance, you miss a day of prayer, Scripture reading, or Scripture memory.[114] But you will not be spiritually prepared when an opportunity presents itself in the future.[115] This is the procrastinator's trouble spot—he is always less prepared than he could have been. Quadrant 2 is where the procrastinator needs to spend more time. It is the quadrant of preparation.

Quadrant 3 is *not important but urgent*. While we must spend some time here, through adequate planning we can spend less. Jesus' dinner with Mary and Martha provides a good example. Dirty dishes have a place, but not first place. Martha's serving may have felt like it needed to be done right away, but when Jesus is seated at your table, the dishes can wait. Giving your undivided attention to the words of Jesus is of greater importance than your acts of service. The procrastinator lives in the *urgent* quadrants. Actually, if you put off anything long enough, it will eventually become urgent and you'll have to do it. But such a pattern keeps you from doing what is really important. Goethe said, "Things which matter most must never be at the mercy of things which matter least."[116]

Finally, there's quadrant 4. These are the items that

are neither important nor urgent. Because the procrastinator has not developed proper priorities, he is prone to spend an inordinate amount of time in this category. Mindlessly surfing the internet, excessive online gaming, entertainment, and social media fill this category. The average young person ages 8-18 spends 44.5 hours of screen time per week.[117] More often than not, this is quadrant 4 activity. When you put off the important (because it isn't urgent) you often replace it with the unimportant. Proverbs 12:11 warns us: "Whoever works his land will have plenty of bread, but he who follows worthless pursuits lacks sense." The word *worthless* can mean empty, unprincipled, or vain.[118] It is used to describe a cistern that is empty of water.[119] It is also used to describe the pursuit of desires that are unfulfilled.[120] It's a good word to describe quadrant 4. Time spent here is a waste of time. Furthermore, worthless desires will always remain unfulfilled—wanting more of your time, no matter how much you give. Most procrastinators find they spend a significant amount of time in quadrant 4. This is why, when a procrastinator claims: *I just didn't have enough time*, they are deceiving themselves. They did have time, they just spent too much of it in quadrant 4.

The procrastinator spends most of his time in quadrants 1, 3, and 4. He allows something or someone to set his priorities with the *urgent* marker (quadrants 1 and 3). Then, as he falls further behind with the important things that he didn't get to, he will give himself to the *unimportant* (quadrant 4). As this pattern continues, the *urgent* list grows longer, and he pushes the *important* issues off until tomorrow. Jesus gave a powerful promise when he said, "But seek first the kingdom of God and his righteousness, and all these things will added unto you."[121] Because God holds you responsible for what you seek to do first,[122] you cannot allow the tyranny of the urgent to set your priorities. To overcome procrastination, you will need to reevaluate your priorities and invest your time in things of lasting value (see pages 70-71 to evaluate your priorities by using the Eisenhower matrix).

(3) Biblicize -- "not as unwise, but as wise"
Am I determining what is truly important from Biblical values?

To overcome procrastination you will need to analyze what you're doing wrong with your time, and you will need to make a list of priorities. But ultimately, you must always remember that you are a steward of time, not its owner. When you begin to see that you are a steward of time, you will treat it differently. Remember, it is God's will we are after, not our own. This is why the apostle warns "Therefore do not be foolish, but understand what the will of the Lord is."[123] Note the second phrase in our time passage: "Look carefully then how you walk, *not as unwise but as wise*, making the best use of the time." [emphasis added].

The Bible speaks a lot about wisdom, and Psalm 90:12 reveals an important step in attaining it: "So teach us to number our days that we may get a heart of wisdom."[124] *The ESV Study Bible* comments:

> This refers especially to the ability to make the most of one's days, since they are so few. The heart of wisdom would enable the faithful to live by the right priorities.[125]

The procrastinator doesn't number his days, he presumes upon them. He isn't counting down the time, he assumes he has more of it. Elizabeth Kubler-Ross once said,

> It is only when we truly know and understand that we have a limited time on earth – and that we have no way of knowing when our time is up – that we will begin to live each day to the fullest, as if it was the only one we had.[126]

This is why the wise person in Psalm 90 is likened to a meticulous accountant. He sees time as a limited resource and will be selective in his investment of his time.

A practical way to "number your days" is to list out your roles of responsibility. These roles require different times and commitments. As an example, these are some of the responsibilities that God has entrusted to me:

- I am a Christian
- I am a husband
- I am a father
- I am an employee (a pastor)
- I am a student
- I am a mentor

These roles are relational; they involve my interaction with others in real time. If you are lazy, you will let others determine the use of your time based upon their perceived needs. When you let others define your roles, you will move from the important and into the realm of the urgent. For instance, the culture (or your church) will tell you what you should do as a Christian. Your boss will tell you what you should do as an employee (which usually means more work with less help). Your spouse will attempt to hold you to their expectations of your weekend, and your kids will make demands on your time morning, noon, and night.

Pop culture counters that with all those demands by others, you need to spend more time on yourself. But this position forgets the truth that time was never yours or theirs. It was a gift from God and should have been used accordingly. This is why simply listing your responsibilities is not sufficient to overcome procrastination. You need to clarify how you are to spend your time in those roles. I have found the Scriptures to be a tremendous help when it comes to defining our roles and responsibilities. Occasionally, you just have to make up a word to get your point across. *Biblicize* is that kind of word. I analyze, I prioritize, and then I biblicize. If I am really serious about doing the will of God, then I will need to get serious about understanding the Word of God. If I don't let the Scriptures inform my specific responsibilities, I will give my time to what others want, and I will revert to procrastinating on the important things that God has called me to do. Notice how even just a handful of Biblical passages help clarify these roles:

- As a Christian *I am to love God and love the people around me* (Mat. 22:36-40)
- As a husband, *I am to love my wife sacrificially* (Eph. 5:25) *and live with her in an understanding way* (1 Pet. 3:7).
- As a father, *I am to instruct my kids in their relationship with the Lord* (Deut. 6:4-7), *discipline them as necessary* (Eph. 6:4), *and avoid provoking them to anger* (Eph. 6:4).
- As an employee (pastor), *I am to spend time in the Word, in prayer* (Acts 6:4; 2 Tim. 4:1-5) *and in community with those in our church* (1 Cor. 12:14-20).
- As a student, *I am to discover and apply God's truths to my life* (Ezra 7:10; Jam. 1:22).
- As a mentor, *I am to seek out, instruct, and encourage the next generation* (1 Tim. 4:13-16; 2 Tim. 2:2).

You are a steward of time, not the owner. As a steward, you first check with the master to see how he wants you to spend your time. This is why we biblicize our roles and responsibilities. When you consider time through the lens of your relationships and roles, you will discover these vital truths:

- *Because time is a limited resource, there will often be a tension between the roles.* Everyone is given 24 hours in a day. Those with whom you have relationships—as defined by your roles—assume that they should have a portion of your 24 hours. However, they're not communicating with one another (it's not their responsibility to), they're just communicating with you. This is the tension you feel. You forget that maintaining a balance between these relationships necessitates a time-tension. You could always spend more time at work, at home, or at church. But time invested in any singular area of our life can create a deficit in another area.

- *Because your roles are relational, some of them have closing windows of opportunity for investment.* If you are a parent, your kids are growing up and moving out.[127] Furthermore, as they reach their young adult years and grow in their independence, your opportunity to instruct them will be in part dependent upon their willingness to receive it. As an employee, there is only so much you can do for your company before retirement. As a spouse, there comes a day when "death will part you."[128] All of our roles have closing windows of opportunity, and these windows are closing at different times. This means that during different seasons of your life you may give more time to one role than another.

This is what it means to *number your days*. As a procrastinator, it feels as if you "always have tomorrow," but when you view life through the lens of your roles and relationships you will see time as a precious commodity. You will not assume the window of opportunity will remain open indefinitely. This is a wakeup call for the procrastinator. If we don't invest our time now in the relationships that are really important, we have no assurance that we'll have more time tomorrow (see pages 72-73 for key Scriptures applied to various roles and responsibilities).

(4) Exercise -- "therefore do not be foolish"
Am I applying self-control with the use of my time?

While analyzing, prioritizing and biblicizing are all necessary steps, walking in the Spirit's power requires application of those truths to your daily decisions. This is the purpose of the phrase in the Ephesians 5:17 passage— "do not be foolish." The fool in the Bible describes the one who should have known better, but did not. Despite being entrusted with the necessary knowledge to change, he stubbornly refused to live differently. He repeatedly did the same thing the same way, but for some reason expected a different result. This is a perfect description of the chronic procrastinator. In the past, he or she may have run out of time to give his or her best effort to the task or relationship, and though they should learn from such history, they sadly repeat the same error and run out of time again.[129] The memory word to help the procrastinator make these necessary changes is the word *exercise*. In order to break his foolish habits, he will need to exercise three elements of self-control.

While self-control may conjure up a self-help kind of mentality, it is actually given by the Holy Spirit, being a part of the fruit of the Spirit:

> But the fruit of the Spirit is love, joy, peace, patience, kindness, goodness, faithfulness, gentleness, *self-control*; against such things there is no law. And those who belong to Christ Jesus have crucified the flesh with its passions and desires [emphasis added].[130]

The Old Testament book of Proverbs adds these warnings: "A man without self-control is like a city broken into and left without walls,"[131] and "A wise man keeps himself under control."[132] Self-control is the mark of the wise, not the foolish. Once the procrastinator has worked through all the steps of discovery mentioned earlier, he will still need to do the hard work of exercising self-control regarding legitimately pursued pleasures. If he doesn't learn to control what he enjoys, he will tend to put off his important priorities and fall back into the habit of procrastination.

Exercise self-control by doing the hardest task first.

Years ago I discovered that, if the first task I chose to do was the one I didn't want to do, I usually had time left over to do the things that I enjoyed. But, if I started with the things that I enjoyed, I never seemed to have the time to do the difficult tasks that I was avoiding. The procrastinator will often choose to do the things he enjoys first and put off the more difficult task for another day. The struggling student plays video games before he studies for tomorrow's test. The stressed out dad races home from work to fit in nine holes at the golf course instead of spending time with his demanding 3-year old son. We tend to do the task we enjoy the most first, and—because we enjoy it—we find that we haven't left sufficient time for the task least preferred. Self-control is needed to take on the hardest task first. I have friends who told their teenage kids, "Always eat the frog first." Spirit-empowered self-control is needed to consistently develop that pattern. A simple way to do this is to make a list of your unfinished tasks, and then, after you have prioritized them, take the one you are least fond of, and move it to the head of the list. Once you have completed the least pleasant task, move on to the others. You will find greater fulfillment in the pleasures you genuinely enjoy when you know that the difficult challenges are behind you, not waiting for you on tomorrow's calendar.

Exercise self-control by doing what you do in moderation.

In his book *Respectable Sins*, author Jerry Bridges describes self-control as follows:

> [Self-control is] control of one's desires, cravings, impulses, emotions and passions. *It is saying no when we should say no. It is moderation in legitimate desires and activities*, and absolute restraint in areas that are clearly sinful [emphasis added].[133]

Time is a limited resource. The wise person understands this truth and practices moderation with those things he legitimately enjoys. The fool does not see the need for moderation. He will binge on the movies he enjoys and push back those unfinished tasks and troubling relationships until tomorrow. The fool believes that time is his own to do with as he pleases. He recoils at the thought of accountability. This is why the Bible teaches that the fool has said in his heart, "there is no God."[134] Sadly, the procrastinator makes the mistake of thinking of himself as sovereign. Until this is corrected, he will never see the need to exercise the activities he enjoys in moderation, and he will push back his responsibilities for another day. To break this habit, you must "learn to say no when you should say no." You must remember that God alone is sovereign. You are a steward of time he has entrusted to you, not the owner. By the Spirit's power, exercise your pleasures in moderation so that you can make the best use of your time to fulfill your God-given responsibilities.

Exercise self-control to persevere when you are discouraged.

Mason Cooley was an American aphorist known for his brief, witty statements. He is reported to have said, "The time I kill is killing me."[135] One of my favorite statements attributed to him was: "Procrastination makes easy things hard and hard things harder."[136] When we procrastinate, it feels as if things just got easier, because we don't have to do the work right now. But in truth we just made a decision that will make tomorrow more difficult than it would have been. When tomorrow arrives, you not only have that day's work, but yesterday's as well. As you push two days of unfinished work into the future, the mountain grows and becomes more difficult to scale. It's easy to see how discouragement can creep in.

When Hurricane Sandy slammed into the New Jersey Coast, our church participated in the cleanup effort. We partnered with *Samaritan's Purse* in helping people restore homes to their previous condition. Atlantic City, New Jersey is built on a barrier island just off the mainland. The storm surge pushed four to six feet of water across the breadth of the island, damaging everything beneath the high-water mark. Marge[137] was an elderly woman on the west side of the island. Our supervisor, having visited the location, warned us that Marge was a hoarder; care would need to be taken to not offend her in the clean up. Marge lived on the second floor of her home because you could not walk through the first floor. Every room was filled with her effects: years' worth of newspapers, clothes, bedding, stuffed animals, and various other possessions sat soaked in Sandy's aftermath. A crew of 25 volunteers worked the entire day, pulling those waterlogged belongings to the curb. I can still remember how hard it was for Marge to make a decision about what to do with her things, even though they were damaged beyond repair. Early on, the decisions were laborious, but her spirits lifted as the day progressed. She seemed younger, more talkative. She smiled as we pulled twenty years of hoarding to the curb for disposal. The local news station interviewed her, and she expressed gratitude to her "new-found friends" who had "done for her what she could not do for herself." Her relief was palpable. Decades of indecision had paralyzed her ability to make a decision.

When the procrastinator keeps pushing back decisions that need to be made, his life becomes overwhelming—like the first floor of Marge's apartment. It's easy to grow discouraged when our failure to make decisions renders our lives a soggy living space overflowing with trash. This is where self-control needs to step in. Don't succumb to your desires, cravings and impulses, no matter how insistent they are about being obeyed. Self-control walks by faith, not by feeling. By taking small steps, it perseveres in the face of discouragement. So don't succumb to that overwhelming feeling. Just get started. Take your first step today.

PRACTICING THE STEWARDSHIP OF TIME

Imagine that everyone was given $506,000 each year. You, as well as your friends, could invest it anyway you wanted. There is only one catch. At the end of the year you have to turn in whatever you didn't spend. It's gone forever. No spending. No investing. Just gone. But not to worry, because the following year you receive another half a million dollars to start again. If this cycle were to continue over your lifetime, you would have received nearly 40 million dollars. That's a lot of money. And you might be tempted to be a bit cavalier in your spending and investing. If you knew more money was coming tomorrow, you wouldn't be so concerned about how you spent it today. Unless, of course, it wasn't your money to do with as you please. Imagine that it was someone else's money that you were asked to invest and that one day there would be an accounting. While we may not receive $506,000 each year to invest on behalf of a client, we are given 506,000 minutes each year to invest on behalf of God. Whatever we don't use disappears from our account never to be seen again. God himself gives us time.[138] Invest it in a way that gives glory to our God, so that you too may one day hear, "Well done good and faithful servant."[139]

Begin doing what you want to do now. We are not living in eternity. We have only this moment, sparkling like a star in our hand—and melting like a snowflake.

Sir Francis Bacon, 1561-1626

How to Apply What You've Learned

The discovery of new truths is the beginning of change, but discovery by itself cannot accomplish real change. To do that, you will need to replace your old habits with new ones, your old ideas with more accurate ones, and your old thoughts with more biblical ones. The final pages of this booklet are dedicated to helping you establish those new habits. Prayer, Scripture and the Holy Spirit were the divine resources that Jesus used, and those same resources are available to you and me today.

(1) Prayer

Whatever the struggle, we have a tendency to see prayer as a panic button—we hit it only when we're in need. Yet, the Bible has over 650 examples of prayer. These are an excellent resource for growth in your prayer life. The following pages offer a prayer pattern and a listing of the names of God.

(2) Scripture

A growing understanding of God's will for us is essential to overcoming procrastination. A daily Bible reading plan—flexible enough for the one just starting to the seasoned reader—is included. To aid with Scripture retrieval, I have included 20 biblical passages to memorize that apply directly to procrastination.

(3) The Spirit

Dependence on the Spirit is essential for overcoming procrastination. Developing new habits by walking in the Spirit is the means through which we express that daily dependence.

The 10 Minute Prayer Pattern: PRAY

The *PRAY* acrostic is a memory device for prayer. It can be as short as a few minutes, or may include more time as God leads. PRAY stands for Praise, Repent, Ask, and Yield.

(1) Praise

At the beginning of prayer, praise the *who*, *what*, and *why* of God. Remember *who* he is by reflecting upon his character. When you remember *what* he's done, you are meditating on his works. Finally, remember the *why* of God. He is motivated by his steadfast love towards us (Psa. 100:5).

(2) Repent

Once you've thought about what God has done, you can move easily to what *you* haven't done. Repentance takes place when we remember our failures and turn from them. A humble confession in prayer reveals a dependence on the Spirit in order to be restored to God. True repentance includes my actions and attitudes (Phil. 2:5).

(3) Ask

Jesus taught us to *ask* of God, and Paul gave us a great prayer list to follow (see Col. 1:9-12). The spiritual nature of the prayers of Scriptures are helpful in praying for yourself and others.

(4) Yield

Jesus grew to the point where he could say, "Not my will but yours be done." Yielding your desires (as hard as that may initially be) is an essential element of prayer. Once you've made known your requests, make sure you surrender your desires.

Reflecting on the Character of God

Praise is an essential part of prayer. An abridged listing of the attributes and names of God follows. Reflecting upon these characteristics of God will enhance your prayer time. This is valuable for the procrastinator who needs to grow in his trust of God.

Able – 2 Tim. 1:12
All Knowing – Psa. 139:1-6
Awesome – Neh. 1:5
Comforter – John 15:26
Conqueror – Rom. 8:35-39
Creator – Gen. 1
Defender – Zech. 9:15
Deliverer – Psalm 18:2
Everlasting Strength - Is. 9:6
Faithful – 1 Cor. 10:13
Forgiving – Psa. 130:4
Friend – Jn. 15:12-16
Glory – Psa. 24:7
God of Hope – Rom. 15:13
Gracious – Psa. 145:8
Great – Dan. 2:45
Guide – Psa. 23:3
Helper – Psa. 46:1
Hiding Place – Psa. 32:7
Holy – Isa. 6:3
Immortal – 1 Tim. 1:17
Infinite – Psa. 147:5
Jealous – Ex. 34:14
Just – Deut. 32:4
King – 1 Tim. 1:17
King of Kings – Rev. 19:16
Lamb of God – Jn. 1:29
Life – Jn. 14:6
Light – Jn. 8:12

Living God – Deut. 5:26
Lord of lords – Rev. 19:16
Love – Rom. 5:8
Majestic – 2 Pet. 1:17
Merciful – Psa. 86:15
Mighty God – Isa. 9:6
Mighty in battle – Psa. 24:8
Most high – Dan. 4:17
Near – Psa. 145:18-21
Omnipresent – Psa. 139:7,8
Omniscient – Psa. 139:1-6
Omnipotent – Job 42:2
Patient – 2 Pet. 3:9
Prince of Peace – Isa. 9:6
Protector – 2 Thes. 3:3
Provider – Heb. 11:40
Redeemer – Job 19:25
Refuge – Psa. 46:1
Rock – Psa. 18:1-2
Savior – Lk. 2:11
Shelter – Psa. 61:4
Strength – Psa. 28:7
Trustworthy – Psa. 84:10-12
Truth – Jn. 8:32, 14:6
Unchanging – Heb. 13:8
Unconquerable – Job 42:2
Victorious – 1 Cor. 15:57
Worthy – Revelation 5:12

From *God's Rx: Alphabet Soup* [141]

Passages about Time

Passages selected for your reading and study.

Time & You	Time & God
Esther 4:14	Genesis 1:1
Psalm 31:15	Genesis 21:33
Psalm 37:18-19	Exodus 3:13-14
Psalm 90:3-6; 10-12	Deuteronomy 33:27
Proverbs 6:6-8; 10-11	Psalm 33:11
Proverbs 16:3, 9	Psalm 90:1-4
Job 10:1-22	Psalm 100:5
Ecclesiastes 3:1-8	Isaiah 57:15
Jeremiah 29:11	Mark 13:32
2 Corinthians 6:2	Galatians 4:4
Ephesians 1:10	Ephesians 3:10-11
Ephesians 5:16	1 Timothy 1:17
James 4:13-15	Revelation 1:8
Philippians 3:13-14	

Passages about Stewardship

We are stewards of time—not owners. The following passage have been selected for their focus on stewardship.

Deuteronomy 8:17-18	1 Corinthians 4:1-2
Psalm 24:1	1 Corinthians 6:19
Psalm 39:4-5	1 Corinthians 9:26-27
Proverbs 13:4	2 Corinthians 8:1-15
Proverbs 16:3	Ephesians 5:15-16
Matthew 5:16	Colossians 4:5-6
Matthew 6:19-21	1 Timothy 4:14-16
Matthew 25:1-46	1 Timothy 6:6-10, 17-19

Reading the Bible: 1-10 chapters per day

The procrastinator struggles to invest his time in the important but non-urgent tasks. He also struggles to prepare a plan to accomplish those tasks. The following Bible reading

Suggestions for Bible reading: 1 to 10 chapters a day

method was developed by Dr. Grant Horner of the English department at The Master's College, Santa Clarita, California. The method is flexible, and can accommodate the beginning to advanced Bible reader.

• Run a copy of the bookmarks on the opposite page; cut them out and place them in your Bible at the various locations.

• The Bible reading is divided into genres for ease of reading. The time frame reflects how many days it will take you to read through that section if you are reading one chapter a day.

• Once you have read the chapter advance the bookmarks through your Bible. When you complete that genre, return the marker to the front of the section and continue reading.

• If you are just starting the habit of Bible reading, choose to read only one or two chapters (for beginners I recommend markers 1 and 7). As you grow in your practice of Bible reading and study, add an additional chapter at one of the markers. Eventually you could easily be reading ten chapters in the Bible a day.

• Ask yourself these questions: (1) What do I see? (2) What does it mean? (3) How should I respond? For more detail on this process see *Just Like Jesus: biblical strategies for growing well*, 64.

• Consider highlighting your Bible as you read. I use green to highlight things God would have me do, red to highlight attitudes or behaviors I am to avoid, and purple to highlight passages that communicate truths about the character or work of God.

• Allow yourself some flexibility in your reading schedule. Everyone has demanding days and missing a chapter here and there shouldn't discourage you from developing the habit of carefully reading your Bible and applying its truth.

Suggestions for Bible reading: 1 to 10 chapters a day

List 1	**Matthew, Mark, Luke, John**	89 days
List 2	**Genesis, Exodus, Leviticus, Numbers, Deuteronomy**	187 days
List 3	Romans, 1 & 2 Corinthians, Galatians, Ephesians, Philippians, Colossians, Hebrews	49 days
List 4	1 & 2 Thessalonians, 1 & 2 Timothy, Titus, Philemon, James, 1 & 2 Peter, 1, 2 & 3 John, Jude, Revelation	65 days
List 5	Job, Ecclesiastes, Song of Solomon	62 days
List 6	**Psalms**	150 days
List 7	**Proverbs**	31 days
List 8	Joshua, Judges, Ruth, 1 & 2 Samuel, 1 & 2 Kings, 1 & 2 Chronicles, Ezra, Nehemiah, Esther	249 days
List 9	Isaiah, Jeremiah, Lamentations, Ezekiel, Daniel, Hosea, Joel, Amos, Obadiah, Jonah, Micah, Nahum, Habakkuk, Zephaniah, Haggai, Zechariah, Malachi	250 days
List 10	**Acts**	28 days

Suggestions for Scripture retrieval: defense & offense

The Scripture Retrieval Method

The Scripture retrieval method is based upon three premises: (1) Scripture provides an excellent *defense* against temptation. This is why the first ten verses listed below are learned in the lie/truth formula to defend against temptation. (2) Scripture provides an excellent *offense* to weaken temptation's appeal. This is why the second ten verses are about the character of God and the nature of the Gospel. Loving God well and appreciating the Gospel weakens the draw of temptation. (3) We learn the Scriptures best when we *understand* the words we are memorizing and *apply* them to our real life challenges. For this reason, memory alone is an ineffective means of defending against sin.

Biblical Truths to Combat the Deceiver's Lies

Lie 1: It's your time. You should be able to use it as you desire. Truth: Ephesians 5:15-16

Lie 2: If you put off what you fear until tomorrow, you will be less anxious. Truth: Psalm 56:3-4

Like 3: If you do the things you should do today, you won't have time for the things you want to do tomorrow. Truth: Proverbs 6:10-11; 13:4;

Lie 4: You won't be able to complete this task if you start it—better not to try. Truth: Philippians 1:6; 4:13

Lie 5: This task is too difficult for you. Wait until it's easier. Truth: Proverbs 3:5, 6

Lie 6: God is not there for you, you'll have to figure this out on your own. Truth: Psalm 73:25-26

Lie 7: You can't change. That's just the way you are. Truth: 2 Corinthians 5:17

Lie 8: Better to live for yourself today; you can start following God tomorrow. Truth: 2 Corinthians 6:2

Lie 9: You'll always have tomorrow to do the things you could do today. Truth: Ecclesiastes 9:10; James 4:14

Lie 10: You'll never resolve this conflict; wait for them to come to you. Truth: Matthew 18:15

Biblical Promises about God and the Gospel

Promise 1: God is in control of time.
  Passage: Psalm 90:2

Promise 2: God loves me and enjoys acting on my behalf.
  Passage: Zephaniah 3:17

Promise 3: My time is short, but God's Word abides forever. Passage: Isaiah 40:7-8

Promise 4: God's grace inspires me to live with diligence Passage: 1 Corinthians 15:10

Promise 5: God is purposefully at work in my life and circumstances. Passage: Jeremiah 29:11, 13

Promise 6: God is sovereign over all.
  Passage: Daniel 4:34-35

Promise 7: God will strengthen me when I am weak.
  Passage: Isaiah 41:10, 13

Promise 8: God's love is sacrificial.
  Passage: John 3:16, 17

Promise 9: God is greater than any difficulty.
  Passage: Jeremiah 32:27

Promise 10: God loved me even when I was unworthy.
  Passage: Romans 5:6-8

Visit biblicalstrategies.com to order these 20 memory verse cards with helpful commentary on the back of each card.

Suggestions for Spirit controlled living: analyze

Analyze: Am I wasting time?

A fifteen minute journal is an excellent way to discover how you are spending your time.

- *Keep your entries simple.* The purpose of journaling is to locate where you can make adjustments to your time.

- *Maintain the entries for 1-2 weeks.* Over the course of several weeks you will be able to see patterns to make adjustments.

- *Evaluate the entries.* Assess how you have spent your time. Have you spent it on what you believe is important (see 70-71)? Does it reinforce your biblicized roles and responsibilities (see 72-73)?

- *Make adjustments to free up time.* You may discover that you used time poorly. You may also gain additional efficiencies by *batching*—putting similar tasks together while working in 25-30 minute increments. God put similar processes together during creation (Genesis 1-2). See the resources tab at biblicalstrategies.com for more information on this process.

Morning Journal

6^{am}	
6^{15}	
6^{30}	
6^{45}	
7^{am}	
7^{15}	
7^{30}	
7^{45}	
8^{am}	
8^{15}	
8^{30}	
8^{45}	
9^{am}	
9^{15}	
9^{30}	
9^{45}	
10^{am}	
10^{15}	
10^{30}	
10^{45}	
11^{am}	
11^{15}	
11^{30}	
11^{45}	

Mid-day Journal

12^{pm}	
12^{15}	
12^{30}	
12^{45}	
1^{pm}	
1^{15}	
1^{30}	
1^{45}	
2^{pm}	
2^{15}	
2^{30}	
2^{45}	
3^{pm}	
3^{15}	
3^{30}	
3^{45}	
4^{pm}	
4^{15}	
4^{30}	
4^{45}	
5^{pm}	
5^{15}	
5^{30}	
5^{45}	

Evening Journal

6^{pm}	
6^{15}	
6^{30}	
6^{45}	
7^{pm}	
7^{15}	
7^{30}	
7^{45}	
8^{pm}	
8^{15}	
8^{30}	
8^{45}	
9^{pm}	
9^{15}	
9^{30}	
9^{45}	
10^{pm}	
10^{15}	
10^{30}	
10^{45}	
11^{pm}	
11^{15}	
11^{30}	
11^{45}	

Suggestions for Spirit controlled living: analyze

Prioritize: Am I investing time in what is truly important?

To better distinguish our priorities, we introduced the Eisenhower Matrix (see page 47). Take a separate sheet of paper and draw the four quadrants. Draw them large enough that you can list your daily activities in the respective boxes, then do so.

important AND urgent	important BUT not urgent
QUADRANT 1	QUADRANT 2
not important BUT urgent	not important AND not urgent
QUADRANT 3	QUADRANT 4

Notice the diagrams on the following page: if you struggle with procrastinating, there's a good chance your life resembles Diagram A. You are spending an inordinate amount of time on things that are neither important nor urgent. The wise individual has learned to make decisions more in line with Diagram B. He fills his life with important but non-urgent tasks. To make this lifestyle shift, take your sheet and cross out items in quadrant 4. As you do so, write in an important/non-urgent task that you ought to do in quadrant 2.

Suggestions for Spirit controlled living: prioritize

important AND urgent	important BUT not urgent
1	2
3	4
not important BUT urgent	not important AND not urgent

Diagram A – the foolish person

important AND Urgent	important BUT not urgent
1	2
3	4
important BUT urgent	not important AND not urgent

Diagram B – the wise person

Biblicize: Am I determining what is truly important from Biblical values?

Suggestions for Spirit controlled living: biblicize

Your Role	Biblical Passages
Ambassador	Pr. 13:17; 2 Co. 5:20; Ep. 6:20; Jn. 20:21
Church Member	1 Co. 12:12-27; Ro. 12:1-8; Ep. 4:12-16
Citizen	Mt. 22:20-22; Ac. 22:25-27; Ep. 2:19, Ph. 3:20
Disciple	Mt. 10:34-38; Mk. 10:17-27; Lu. 9:23-27; 14:27
Employee	Ge. 2:15; 3:17-19; Pr. 21:25; 1 Th. 2:9; Co. 2:23
Employer	Pr. 22:16; Je. 22:13; Ep. 6:9; Ja. 5:4
Example	1 Co. 11:1; Ro. 14:1-21; 1 Th. 1:5-7; 1 Ti. 4:12
Friend	Pr. 17:17; 27:17; 18:24; Jn. 15:13; Ph. 2:3-8
Husband	Ge. 2:18, 24; Ep. 5:25-33; Co. 3:19; 1 Pe. 3:7
In-law	Ge. 2:24; Ex. 18:1-27; Ru. 1-4
Leader	Mk. 10:42-45; Ph. 2:5-8; 1 Ti. 4:12; 2 Ti. 2:2-26
Man	Jos. 1:8; Ep. 6:1-13; 1 Co. 6;13-14; 1 Jo. 2:6
Neighbor	Pr. 3:29; Mt. 7:12; Lk. 10:25-37; Ro. 15:2; Ja. 2:8
Parent	De. 6:6-9; Ps. 127:3; Pr. 13:24; Co. 3:21; He. 12
Peace keeper	Ps. 34:13-14; Mt. 5:9; He. 12:14; Ja. 3:17-18
Servant	Mt. 25:35-40; Mk. 10:44-45; Ga. 5:13-14
Steward	De. 8:17-18; Mt. 25:14-30; 1 Co. 4:2; 1 Pt. 4:10
Sufferer	Is. 53:3-10; Ac. 9:16; He. 12:2; 1 Pe. 4:12-16; 5:10
Teacher	Ez. 7:10; Lk. 6:40; Ja. 3:1; Tit. 2:7; 2 Ti. 2:24-26
Temple	Ro. 12:1; 1 Co. 3:16-17; 6:19-20; 1 Ti. 4:7-9
Wife	Ge. 2:18; 1 Pe. 3:1-6; Pr. 18:22; 31:10-31
Woman	Ru. 3:11; Pr. 14:1; 31:30; Titus 2:3-5; 1 Pe. 3:1-6

* Neither the roles nor the biblical passages are a comprehensive listing; they are intended to get you started in the identity process.

Developing your identity from Biblical values

- *Seek God's direction through prayer.*

Start by talking to God. He desires for you to trust him and seek his guidance (Pro. 3:5-6). He wants you to know his will so that you might do it (1 Thes. 4:1-3). Focus on an attitude of submission; you want to do whatever he reveals (Mark 14:36).

- *Ponder your roles and responsibilities.*

Think about the roles and responsibilities to which God has called you (review pages 50-52). Most often these will be expressed in the context of your relationships (friend, employee, mother, daughter, etc.). List them. They will become the foundation for the next step.

- *Discover key Scriptures that inform your identity.*

I recommend these tools to find key Biblical passages: a topical Bible, concordance, *The Treasury of Scripture Knowledge*, or *The Quick Scripture Reference for Counseling*. You can also search the internet by entering "What does the Bible say about (fill in your role)."

- *Develop identity statements based upon what you discover when studying Scripture.*

Try to delineate your role to one sentence or it may simply be 3-5 key words. Keeping it concise is the first step to making it memorable. It will need to be memorable if you are to apply it in daily decision-making (see page 52).

- *Make decisions in light of your identity statements.*

Before you commit to a new task or responsibility, check your identity statements. Does this decision fall in line with what God has called you to do? Does it enhance your Biblically derived identity or distract from it? Review the identity statements often, until you've developed the habit of living by them.

NOTES

1. Hebrews 4:12
2. Matthew 25:25
3. James 4:13
4. Proverbs 6:6-8
5. Matthew 25:14-30

6. Don Stewart, "Stewardship" in *The Holman Illustrated Bible Dictionary* (Nashville, TN: Holman Bible Publishers, 2003), 1534.

7. In J.R. Tolkien's *Return of the King*, Lord Denethor is called the *steward* of Gondor, he is not the king. In the Great Hall, the throne from which Denethor rules sits at the base of the stairs that leads to the king's throne; the king's throne is empty at the top of the dais. Tolkien's image captures the idea of stewardship perfectly. In the king's absence, Denethor is to lead the people and protect the kingdom, but he is not to ascend the stairs and take the king's role. He is simply a steward; he has not been granted sovereign authority.

8. John MacArthur, *The MacArthur Study Bible* (Wheaton, IL: Crossway Books, 1997), 2199.

9. Matthew 25:21, 23
10. Matthew 25:24-25
11. Genesis 3:10
12. Genesis 31:31
13. Job 32:6
14. Daniel 8:17, NKJV

15. If you had grown up in Israel during Biblical times you would have experienced fear in an uncertain future firsthand. Your friends and family were torn from their homes and carried into captivity. Even if you were able to stay in your own home, thieves and robbers were constantly on the loose, taking what wasn't theirs and using force with any who opposed. Jesus spoke to that audience when he said, "Therefore do not be anxious about tomorrow, for tomorrow will be anxious for itself. Sufficient for the day is its own trouble." (Matt. 6:34). This is a valuable lesson for the procrastinator: If you put today's trouble off until tomorrow you'll have both tomorrow's trouble and today's as well.

16. Matthew 25:25
17. Proverbs 3:5
18. Judges 7:20
19. 1 Samuel 17:45
20. Matthew 25:15
21. Exodus 13:17
22. Exodus 13:17-18

23. Wayne Grudem, *Systematic Theology: An Introduction to Biblical Doctrine* (Grand Rapids, MI: Intervarsity Press; Zondervan Publishing House, 1994), 189.

24. See *Dead-End Desire: biblical strategies for overcoming self-pity*, 37-47.

25. 1 John 4:18

26. This is one of the reasons that each of the Biblical Strategies booklets includes memory verses on the character of God and the nature of the Gospel. It's not enough to say "no" to the temptation; we must also learn to say "yes" to the truth that God had loved us when we were estranged from him.

27. 1 John 3:16-17; 1 Corinthians 5:17
28. Romans 5:8
29. James 4:6, 10
30. James 5:16
31. James 1:6
32. Proverbs 3:5-6
33. Philippians 2:5
34. Ephesians 2:8-9
35. Matthew 25:15
36. 1 Corinthians 10:13
37. Matthew 25:24-25

38. The Greek word *ginosko* translated here as *know* can also be translated as *perceived*. See Matthew 21:45; Mark 12:12; 15:10. Our perceptions are often slippery. They feel so true, but they can be either accurate or inaccurate.

39. Matthew 25:24

40. Even when his master repeats the phrase it seems to be more of a theoretical question meant to show the inconsistency of the unwise stewards reasoning rather than an acknowledgment of fact.

41. Matthew 25:21, 23

42. I highly recommend a lesson given by Dr. Nicholas Ellen where he speaks of the underlying sin beneath our confident assertions in our perceptions as pride. Available at biblicalstrategies.com under the resource tab.

43. The unwise steward was afraid. Fear is often the motivator for putting difficult tasks off. Perhaps we're afraid of failure or what others might think of us. This perpetrator works in secret, because rarely do we confess it to others until it is too late. How much better to confess our fears, seek help early on, and then walk by faith.

44. http://en.wikipedia.org/wiki/First_inauguration_of_Franklin_D._Roosevelt

45. 1 Corinthians 13:4-8

46. 1 John 4:18

47. 1 John 4:7-9

48. http://www.inspirational-quotes-and-quotations.com/quotes-by-robert-kiyosaki.html

49. http://thinkexist.com/quotation/work_while_it_is_called_today-or_you_know_not/146135.html

50. Matthew 6:34

51. Matthew 18:15

52. Ephesians 5:26-27

53. Eugene Peterson, *The Message: The Bible in Contemporary Language* (Colorado Springs, CO: NavPress, 2005), Ephesians 4:27.

54. James 4:13-16

55. Jeremiah 29:11

56. Luke 14:28

57. Galatians 6:9

58. If we take a bird's eye view of the four gospels, we see Jesus understanding of the brevity of time. For instance, in his three preaching expeditions into Galilean countryside, he first goes alone (Luke 4:14), then he calls the 12 disciples, and takes them with him (Luke 6:12-19), finally, he divides them in groups of twos and sends them out two-by-two into the Galilean countryside - multiplying his preaching and healing ministry six-fold (Luke 9:1-6). There seems to be a sense of increased urgency regarding his final days in Galilee and his need to get the message out. Upon his leaving the Galilean communities, he begins a private training of the disciples (Matthew 16:13) in preparation for his impending death, resurrection, and departure. Luke captures this focus with the words "he set his face towards Jerusalem" (Luke 9:51; 13:22). What makes Jesus' ministry fascinating is that he never seems rushed in his conversations with individuals, yet he accomplishes so much in less than four years of public and private ministry. He doesn't procrastinate.

59. Romans 12:11

60. Romans 12:16

61. http://news.bbc.co.uk/earth/hi/earth_news/newsid_8100000/8100876.stm

62. Proverbs 6:6

63. W.E. Vine, *Vine's Expository Dictionary of New Testament Words* (Mclean, VA: Macdonald Publishing, 1989), 284.

64. Consider the life of Jesus. When he informed the disciples he would be leaving shortly he promised them that he was going to prepare a place for them (John 14:2), and then he would return. Christians have been waiting for two millennia for his return, and still find encouragement in the truth that Jesus left us here on earth and went to prepare a place for us.

65. Genesis 37:28

66. Genesis 39:6-23

67. Genesis 41:1-14
68. Genesis 41:38
69. Genesis 41:28-31
70. Psalm 90:2
71. Genesis 37:2; 41:46
72. Genesis 40:7
73. Genesis 40:8
74. Joseph had grown in his humility and shows remarkable growth when interpreting the dreams of the cupbearer and baker (Gen. 40:1-22). In his earlier dream (Gen. 37:5-11), he makes no mention of God and appears to lack humility in the sharing of it.
75. http://thinkexist.com/quotation/procrastination_is_opportunity_natural_assassin/259965.html
76. James 4:13-17
77. Genesis 41:34–36
78. Genesis 47:25
79. Genesis 41:32
80. John 12:27
81. Luke 9:51
82. John 12:32
83. R.H. Stein, *Vol. 24: Luke. The New American Commentary* (Nashville: Broadman & Holman Publishers, 1992), 298.
84. http://www.desiringgod.org/sermons/he-set-his-face-to-go-to-jerusalem
85. Mark 14:36
86. Christ's face was set toward Jerusalem, and Luke's narrative is a travelogue of that long journey to the cross. This was a dramatic turning point in Christ's ministry. After this, Galilee was no longer His base of operation. Although [Luke] 17:11–37 describes a return visit to Galilee, Luke included everything between this point and that short Galilean sojourn as part of the journey to Jerusalem. We know from a comparison of the gospels that, during this period of Christ's ministry, He made short visits to Jerusalem to celebrate feasts (see notes on 13:22; 17:11). Nonetheless, those brief visits were only interludes in this period of ministry that would culminate in a final journey to Jerusalem for the purpose of dying there. Thus Luke underscored this turning point in Christ's ministry more dramatically than any of the other gospels, by showing Christ's determination to complete His mission of going to the cross (John MacArthur, *The MacArthur Study Bible* (Wheaton, IL: Crossway Books, 1997), 1533).

87. Luke 18:31-33
88. Matthew 16:21-22
89. Jerome Smith, *The New Treasury of Scripture Knowledge* (Nashville, TN: Thomas Nelson Publishers, 1992), 1168.
90. Luke 17:5
91. http://procrastinus.com/procrastination/procrastination-quotes/
92. John 12:27
93. John 12:32-33
94. John 12:28
95. Mark 10:44-45
96. John MacArthur, *The MacArthur Study Bible* (Wheaton, IL: Crossway Books, 1997), 1033.
97. Psalm 37:3, 4, 5, 7
98. John 14:2, 3
99. Ironically, when we put off today's task until a short-term tomorrow (time on earth), we are not thinking clearly in terms of the long-term tomorrow (time in eternity).
100. "Jesus allowed himself to be led by the Spirit. Anyone following Christ will do the same. Luke records, 'And Jesus, full of the Holy Spirit, returned from the Jordan and was led by the Spirit in the wilderness' (Luke 4:1). In the 5th chapter of Galatians, Paul gives four commands that capture this same idea. Each is uniquely associated with walking. He says we are to: be led by the Spirit; walk in the Spirit;

live by the Spirit; and keep in step with the Spirit (Gal. 5:16, 18, 25) This is instructive; walking is the biblical metaphor to describe daily habits. John MacArthur explains, 'The fact that *peripateō* (walk) is used here in the present tense indicates that Paul is speaking of continuous, regular action, in other words, a habitual way of life. And the fact that the verb is also in the imperative mood indicates he is not giving believers an option but a command. Among other things, walking implies progress, going from where one is to where he ought to be. As a believer submits to the Spirit's control, he moves forward in his spiritual life. Step by step the Spirit moves him from where he is toward where God wants him to be'"(Phil Moser, *Just Like Jesus*, 43).

101. Ephesians 5:15-18

102. Luke 1:3; Matthew 2:8; Acts 23:15; Acts 18:26

103. A conversation with Randy Patten, Director of Training and Development for the Association of Certified Biblical Counselors.

104. Theologian Paul Enns summarizes the Biblical meaning of redemption in this way: "The word redemption comes from the Greek word *agorazo* and means 'to purchase in the marketplace.' Frequently it had to do with the sale of slaves in the marketplace. The word is used to describe the believer being purchased out of the slave market of sin and set free from sin's bondage. The purchase price for the believer's freedom and release from sin was the death of Jesus Christ (1 Cor. 6:20; 7:23; Rev. 5:9; 14:3, 4) [...] A second word related to the believer's redemption is *exagorazo*, which teaches that Christ redeemed believers from the curse and bondage of the law that only condemned and could not save. Believers have been purchased in the slave market (*agorazo*) and removed from (*ex*) the slave market altogether. Christ set believers free from bondage to the law and from its condemnation (Gal. 3:13; 4:5) [...] A third term that is used to explain redemption is *lutroo* which means "to obtain release by the payment of a price." The idea of being set free by payment of a ransom is prevalent in this word (Luke 24:21). Believers have been redeemed by the precious blood of Christ (1 Pet. 1:18) to be a special possession for God (Titus 2:14)" (Paul Enns, *The Moody Handbook of Theology* (Chicago, IL: Moody Press, 1989).

105. Luke 10:38-42

106. R.H. Stein, *Vol. 24: Luke. The New American Commentary* (Nashville: Broadman & Holman Publishers, 1992), 321.

107. Address to the Century Association, December 7, 1961.

108. The matrix appears to have grown out of Eisenhower's statement, but there is no evidence that he personally developed it. A special thanks to Mary Burtzloff, Archivist, Eisenhower Presidential Library and Museum for her helpful research on my behalf in this matter.

109. Important and urgent (Luke 10:30,33). Important but not urgent (Matt. 6:33). Not important but urgent (Luke 10:40-41). Not important and not urgent (Prov. 12:11).

110. Luke 10:30, 33

111. Mark 1:36

112. Luke 4:1-15

113. Luke 4:14-30

114. See *Just Like Jesus; biblical strategies for growing well* for these

important elements of the Christian life.

115. This is why Scripture memory is an integral part of each Biblical Strategies booklet. You will not have immediate access to key biblical passages when the pressure is on unless you had memorized when there was no pressure.

116. http://thinkexist.com/quotation/things_which_matter_most_must_never_be_at_the/180010.html

117. http://www.ikeepsafe.org/be-a-pro/balance/too-much-time-online/

118. James Strong, *The New Strong's Dictionary of Hebrew and Greek Words* (Nashville, TN: Thomas Nelson, 1996).

119. Genesis 37:24

120. Isaiah 29:8

121. Matthew 6:33

122. Matthew 6:33

123. Ephesians 5:17

124. Psalm 90:12

125. *The ESV Study Bible* (Wheaton, IL: Crossway Bibles, 2008), 1053.

126. http://thinkexist.com/quotation/it-s_only_when_we_truly_know_and_understand_that/205489.html

127. Genesis 2:24

128. Matthew 19:6

129. Proverbs 26:11

130. Galatians 5:22-23

131. Proverbs 25:28

132. Proverbs 29:11

133. Jerry Bridges, *Respectable Sins* (Colorado Springs, CO: NavPress, 2007).

134. Psalm 14:1

135. http://en.wikipedia.org/wiki/Mason_Cooley

136. http://www.brainyquote.com/quotes/quotes/m/masoncoole396387.html

137. This is not her real name.

138. Ephesians 5:16

139. Psalm 139:16

140. Matthew 25:23

141. Nancy Adels, *God's RX: Alphabet Soup*, 15-107.

About Biblical Strategies

Biblical Strategies exists to provide resources for those who desire to change, but need help taking the next steps.

- The series is comprised of brief booklets that explain and apply Biblical passages to a specific struggle.
- The accountability plan helps the reader overcome the temptation by implementing the key growth habits of prayer, Scripture memory, daily Bible readings, and application of truth.
- The Scripture Retrieval System is a memory aid in which Biblical passages have been selected for each temptation. Ten passages expose temptation's deception; the remainder weaken temptation's appeal as truths about the character of God and the nature of the gospel are committed to memory.

About 12th Man Training

12th Man Training is character-based instruction for men using the Biblical Strategies material. Biblical help is offered in 30, twenty-minute teaching segments as men develop biblical strategies for overcoming the issues with which they often struggle — anger, self-pity, sexual temptation, procrastination, anxiety, and broken relationships. These sessions are offered for free online. Go to the blog at biblicalstrategies.com and select 12th Man Training.

A unique aspect of the training is the directed table-talk discussions. For 35 minutes following the teaching, a table leader fosters discussion around that week's topic, provides accountability for each man's spiritual growth, and builds community among the men at the table.

About the Author

Phil Moser is the author of the Biblical Strategies series. He is a pastor, frequent blogger (philmoser.com) and conference speaker. He holds a degree in Business Management, and earned his Masters of Divinity from The Master's Seminary, Sun Valley, California. He presently serves as the teaching pastor of Fellowship Bible Church in Mullica Hill, New Jersey. He has served as an adjunct professor teaching the Bible, theology, apologetics, homiletics, and counseling in Albania, Korea, Germany, Hungary and Ukraine.

Resources from Biblical Strategies

Just Like Jesus: biblical strategies for growing well

Fighting the Fire: biblical strategies for overcoming anger

Dead End Desire: biblical strategies for overcoming self-pity

Taking Back Time: biblical strategies for overcoming procrastination

Safe in the Storm: biblical strategies for overcoming anxiety

Discerning the Deception: biblical strategies for overcoming sexual temptation

Biblical Strategies
How you get to where God's taking you.
BiblicalStrategies.com